AND I WILL BLESS
THOSE WHO BLESS YOU
GENESIS 12:3

A CELEBRATION OF CHRISTIAN *sacrificial giving*
TO ISRAEL AND THE JEWISH PEOPLE

And I Will Bless Those Who Bless You

Copyright © 2008 by International Fellowship of Christians & Jews, Inc.
All rights reserved.

Unless otherwise noted, all quotations are taken from the *Holy Bible, New International Version*®. Copyright © 1973, 1978, 1984 by International Bible Society. Used by permission.

Published by International Fellowship of Christians & Jews, Inc.
30 North LaSalle St., Suite 2600, Chicago, IL 60602-3356

ISBN 978-0-9816577-2-1
First printing: February 2009

And I Will Bless
Those Who Bless You
GENESIS 12:3

A CELEBRATION OF CHRISTIAN *sacrificial giving*
TO ISRAEL AND THE JEWISH PEOPLE

INTERNATIONAL FELLOWSHIP OF CHRISTIANS AND JEWS™

DEDICATION

To the millions of our Christian friends around the world who love Israel and the Jewish people. May you reap a bountiful harvest for every righteous seed you have so generously sown.

CONTENTS

Introduction IX
Helping His Fellow Man: *George Lancia / Svetlana* 16
Fueled by Compassion: *Marlon & Tammy Weaver / Lubya* 20
Giving Back: *Karen Moody / Ina* 24
New Priorities: *Tedd & Jacki Rhodes / Marat* 28
Scriptures 32
Listening for His Voice: *Priscilla Wolfe / Miriam* 34
A Special Way to Remember: *John & Deborah Harvison / Sagu* 38
Riding High: *Kathy Sullivan / Paul* 42
A Bishop's Love for Israel: *Jason Sanderson / Mark* 46
Scriptures 50
Leap of Faith: *Mike & Kenna Day / Bogeh* 52
We Came to Love Them through the Bible: *Bruce & Lavetta Pople / Rivka* ... 56
A Friend for Life: *Irina Azar / Alem* 60

Like Father, Like Son: *Robert Fulton / Andre* 64

Scriptures 68

Providence at Every Turn: *Barbara Walker / Fira* 70

Influencing Minds and Hearts: *Beth & Arthur McInnis / Sasha* 74

Giving from a Full Heart: *Evelyn Betita / Ovadiah* 78

Putting Conviction into Action: *Troy & Elisa Blaylock / Doron & Motti* 82

Scriptures 86

A Special Bond: *John & Sheila Rollow / Vadim* 88

A Heart for Giving: *Dianne Kessler-Bosak / Eugene* 92

Being a Part of History: *John & Jennifer Rainney / Sophie* 96

Called to Give and Pray: *Sandy Fox / Marcos & Zola* 100

Scriptures 104

Fulfilling God's Purposes: *Varitema Nassau / Victor* 106

Inspiring a Legacy of Love: *David & Dianna Shipley / Ziv* 110

Adopted into God's Family: *Charlotte Karl / Victoria* 114

A Family Affair: *Scott Sears & Dana Kent / Marko* 118

Giving and Receiving: *Jay & Jo Anne Gould / Misha* 122

Scriptures 126

INTRODUCTION

God's Children—Together Again

It is a privilege for me to celebrate with you twenty-five years of building bridges of understanding between Christians and Jews and to thank you for your cooperation in standing in solidarity with Israel and the Jewish people. In the pages of this book, you will find stories of some of our Christian partners alongside short narratives describing individuals whose life-saving dreams came true because of your generous support. We hope these accounts will inspire and encourage you as you witness the fruits of our laboring together in this groundbreaking fellowship of Jews and Christians.

I am grateful for the support of our hundreds of thousands of partners who have contributed to *The Fellowship* over the past twenty-five years. I am deeply humbled by the number of people who have given sacrificially, often foregoing their own needs and desires in order to bless Israel and offer a better life to Jews who otherwise would have no hope.

I'm often asked, "How did you begin the *International Fellowship of Christians and Jews*—what motivated you?"

I attribute it to an event that happened some twenty-five years ago when I visited Israel for the first time together with a group of Christians. My roommate on the tour was an eighty-six-year-old African American Baptist minister from Virginia.

The first day, in a quiet moment alone, I remember walking onto my hotel room veranda, which overlooked the beautiful city of Jerusalem. As I began to pray, I was overcome with the emotion of the moment. I thought, *I'm here! I'm praying to G-d right here in my homeland, the very center of the universe.*

After a long day, I returned late to my room. As I entered quietly, I observed what would change my life forever.

My roommate was kneeling at his bed, his arms outstretched to heaven while he repeated these words: "Lord, Lord! Thank You. I am luckier than Moses. Moses only got to see the Promised Land, but I have been able to walk in it before I die."

At that moment, I realized something that had never occurred to me before: *This twenty-five-year-old, white rabbi from New York and this elderly African American minister from Virginia have far more in common than I ever imagined—our tears and thanksgiving to G-d for "bringing us home."* I believe that very moment was the point when I felt "called" by G-d to fulfill the mission of building bridges of healing, understanding, and reconciliation between Jews and Christians, transcending the gulf that has existed between our faith communities for 2,000 years. It is time to reverse the sad and tragic history of fratricide and deep-seated enmity that has kept us separated for far too long.

It's been an amazing journey. I've seen this organization grow from a one-room office with two employees (I was one!) to having two offices and a staff of over ninety employees. This astonishing growth—that has taken place despite the many claims that this ministry was "too controversial" to succeed—was made possible by none other than you, our partners and friends, along with the blessing and direction of G-d. Your faith in G-d, your heartfelt, continual prayers, your persistent giving, and your unabashed love for the Jewish people have brought *The Fellowship* to where it is today.

Together, we are helping make possible the prophetic *aliyah* of Jewish émigrés in danger. In addition, we are caring for elderly Jews and Jewish orphans in the former Soviet Union, assisting with Israel's protection and provision for the state's poorest families and individuals, and building strong advocates worldwide for Israel. It is truly astounding what G-d has done in these twenty-five years as we have labored together. Today, the strength of *The Fellowship* is a reflection of the strength of our joint faith in the Bible and in the G-d who promised to bless those who bless His people.

This book contains stories of people who have been directly impacted by your support. Because of limited space, we only relayed the basic facts of each story—hardly doing these moving accounts justice.

My daughter, Yael, has had the unique privilege of meeting some of the people who were touched and blessed by your giving. To portray the deep impact you are having on the Jewish people, I would like to share with you one of Yael's recent encounters.

While traveling in Yokne'am, Israel, Yael happened to see a *Fellowship* van. Excited to have spotted it, she asked the driver to stop so that she could take some pictures to send back to us. The driver took that unique opportunity to tell her about the many children who use the bus to get to and from their desperately-needed cancer treatments, the elderly who would otherwise have no means to get to their doctors, and the families who use it to carry groceries to their homes.

But there was one story in particular that the driver wanted to share. Dina, a forty-five-year-old, mentally disabled woman, was left in a hospital in Tel Aviv when she was only three days old. After weeks in a state-run orphanage, Dina was taken in by the Cohens, a couple who survived the Holocaust but couldn't have children of their own. Three years later, they adopted her sister, Aliza. The faithful couple raised their two girls, showering them with love and providing Dina the many therapies she needed to have the best life possible. Aliza got married and moved a block away from her parents to start her own family. Dina remained with the Cohens until three years ago, when they died.

She was soon transported to a state institution for handicapped women where she could receive the care she needed. But being far away from Aliza began to take an emotional toll on Dina—neither sister could visit the other because they lived in different towns and had no money for the commute. In desperation, the state-run institution finally contacted *The Fellowship*, asking if there was any way we could help reunite the siblings on a regular basis. We immediately agreed to take Dina to Aliza's home once a month for Shabbat and to take her back to the institution after the weekend.

At that point, the driver described the monthly trips to Yael. "Every time Dina gets on the bus," he said, "she laughs and sings the whole trip, thanking me profusely for taking her to visit her beloved sister—the only family she has left."

My heart is full of gratitude to G-d as I reflect on how your steadfast love has impacted the lives of Dina and Aliza, as well as countless other Israelis and Jews around the world who face daily struggles to survive. Your unwavering commitment is a powerful demonstration of the words of Psalm 133:1: *"How good and pleasant it is when brothers live together in unity!"*

May the G-d of Abraham, Isaac and Jacob, Sarah, Rebecca, Rachel and Leah bless you, His children—Christians grafted into the rich olive tree of Israel—for blessing His people, Israel (Genesis 12:3).

With prayers for *shalom*, peace,
Rabbi Yechiel Eckstein

International Fellowship of Christians and Jews

HELPING HIS FELLOW MAN

George Lancia, California

GEORGE LANCIA LIVES and works in one of the most beautiful seaside cities in America. This man knows the hilly terrain of his eclectic urban paradise like the back of his own hand; he has to—he's been a cab driver in San Francisco for over thirty years.

A single man in his fifties, George makes a decent income for himself, but he chooses to live simply. "My life-goal is to help my fellow man," relates the cabbie with his trademark directness and optimism. "When I see someone who needs help, I have to act," he says. "I understand that the Jewish people have endured a long history of persecution, and I want to do something about it."

George keeps the flag of Israel and the Star of David over his meter in his cab. "I love the Jewish people," he says with delight, "and I love doing God's will by blessing them, even if it seems like something small."

For example, the seasoned cab driver has an unusual policy regarding cab fare for Israeli citizens who are on personal travel in the United States: the ride from the airport to the city is free of charge. He gets some flack from his fellow drivers who say they could never afford to do such a thing. George finds the opposite to be true. "When you make these little sacrifices, it never fails that, in time, God rewards you. It may not be the next day, but the Lord always comes through. I often receive a large tip later on, or some other unexpected blessing."

Over eight years ago, George, an avid history buff and fan of documentaries, was deeply moved by the persecution the Jews suffered under the Nazis. He says, "I vowed if I ever had the opportunity to help the Jewish people, I would do it. I especially have a big heart for those living in Russia. You never know when the doors will close. We need to help while there is still opportunity. The last time they closed, it was for seventy years."

A year ago, George's opportunity to help Russian Jews came in a big way. After supporting *The Fellowship* for over seven years as best he could on his cab-driving income, George was blessed by a family inheritance. "I began using some of the funds myself, and then I realized this was my once-in-a-lifetime chance to really make an impact. God gave the Jewish people Israel, fulfilling His promise that they would have a homeland of their own. God promises to bless those who bless Israel," he says. "How could I not help them get there? It's like giving a family a whole new lease on life."

George made a decision to give a significant portion of his inheritance to *The Fellowship*. When asked if this was a difficult decision, he didn't hesitate to answer. "No, no, no! It was very pleasant. Very happy."

One can only imagine how "very happy" a Jewish family living in Russia will be upon returning to their homeland—all because of a soft-hearted cab driver in San Francisco.

Svetlana, Israel

Svetlana and Iro had big dreams of moving to Israel together. "When we were in high school, instead of going out, we would stay home and plan our fantasy life there... even though we had no means to make the journey," Svetlana shares.

After the couple married, a pregnant and very determined Svetlana found out about *The Fellowship's On Wings of Eagles* program. But before they were able to make *aliyah* (immigrate to Israel), she lost both parents, and later her husband.

Svetlana remembers her flight to Israel with her daughter Irina: "I felt like I was bringing with me the members of my family who had tragically passed. My mother and father were on that plane, and I know my husband was, too. This was our dream. I knew I wasn't going alone."

Svetlana is looking forward to working in Israel and to giving Irina the Jewish education she always dreamed of.

International Fellowship of Christians and Jews

FUELED BY COMPASSION

Marlon and Tammy Weaver, South Carolina

Marlon and Tammy Weaver have made a home together in the southern seaside community of Myrtle Beach, South Carolina. "I've been a country boy all of my life," says Marlon, "but when I discovered the city, and especially the ocean, it became my dream to live here."

The owner of a highway and road construction business, Marlon describes his entrepreneur wife, Tammy, as his "perfect match." Then he laughs and quickly adds, "But we're total opposites!" Tammy started the first day spa in booming Myrtle Beach and boasts thirty-five years of experience in the field.

The couple's individual faith journeys were ignited by personal tragedy. Marlon's loving mother lost her life at the hands of local hoodlums when they robbed her marina store for a small sum. The irony was that his mom had known the thieves when they were boys. "I had to learn to forgive," says Marlon. "It wasn't easy, but it was the only way to get on with life." It was during that time that he became serious about his faith, and he's never looked back since.

Years later, Marlon and Tammy married. It was the second marriage for each. Marlon had three daughters and Tammy had a son, Harley, with whom Marlon enjoyed a close relationship. "Harley was a fun-loving young man, and helped me out at our company," recalls Marlon warmly. "One day when he was about twenty years old, we closed early due to rain. Harley decided to have some fun in the mud on his ATV on our farmland near the office." The fun took a tragic turn as he ran into a tree and never recovered. "It was truly devastating," relays Marlon.

At a loss for how to comfort the love of his life, Marlon bought Tammy a Bible with comments and explanations for her to read and understand. "She took that Bible out to the farm every single day. Eventually, she found some peace and the strength to go on," he recalls. Tammy still reads her Bible daily.

The Weavers' tragedies brought them to a closer personal relationship with God. While their own suffering has made their hearts tender toward others who have experienced pain, it is their love of the scriptures that led them to embrace the Jewish people.

One day, the Weavers saw a *Fellowship* presentation on television. "This was during the time when Israel was being bombarded by Hamas and Hezbollah," Marlon remembers. "I told Tammy, 'These people need our help!'" Tammy was in total agreement, so they became steadfast partners, faithfully sending monthly gifts.

The couple also visited Israel with *The Fellowship*, and Marlon was baptized in the Jordan River. "It's a beautiful country," he remarks. "It's surrounded by mountains and is so fertile that just about anything will grow there. The people are very intelligent, too."

"It is so clear to us that God has blessed the Israeli people in a special way. He has a big plan for this tiny country," says Marlon. "Tammy and I came to understand that the Jews are God's chosen people. The Bible promises us that He will bless those who bless them. We want to make sure we do our part in standing with them and seeing God's plan for them come to pass."

Lyuba, Israel

Lyuba, a lovely, soft-spoken seventeen-year-old girl from Ukraine, was abandoned by her father at age seven. Years later, her mother was murdered. Forced to live on the streets even during brutal Ukrainian winters, Lyuba survived. And then, it seemed to her a miracle began. Relatives in Israel heard of Lyuba's plight and contacted *The Fellowship*'s colleagues in Ukraine. They found Lyuba and flew her to Israel "*On Wings of Eagles.*"

She was warmly welcomed at *Migdal Ohr* (Tower of Light), a *Fellowship*-funded children's school and community that provides shelter, education, and guidance to 6,000 orphaned or abandoned children.

Lyuba now faces her future with new hope and determination.

International Fellowship of Christians and Jews

GIVING BACK

Karen Moody, Missouri

KAREN MOODY IS a woman who has persevered in spite of formidable life-challenges. A single mother stricken with fibromyalgia, Karen has struggled financially for most of her adult life. It took quite a long time before she was able to have her illness diagnosed and treatment implemented that would eventually bring some relief.

Karen's son, Canyon, was an extremely bright and creative child. For many years, the small family relied on public assistance. Through it all, Karen invested herself heavily in raising her son well by keeping his active mind engaged and igniting his spiritual growth. "We were so blessed to have a family that was there for us," recalls Karen. "My parents, my brother, and my sister helped pull us through many struggles."

As the years went by and Canyon grew to be a young teenager, things began to shift for the better in Karen's finances. She tithed and gave to ministries, and God began pulling her out of financial distress. Eventually, she was able to move out of low-income housing and off public assistance. Shortly after getting her first sales job, Karen was moved by Rabbi Eckstein's television appeal on behalf of Russian Jews who desperately needed funding to make *aliyah*. "My heart was heavy when I saw how they lived and the persecution they endured," relays Karen. As she stepped out in faith, listening to God "direct her" in giving to the Jewish people, Karen's life and sales career blossomed well beyond her dreams.

While working at a telecommunications company, Karen set sales records so high that her employers capped her commissions. Having a burning desire to "give back to others," the single mother kept giving larger amounts to *The Fellowship*, some even disproportionate to her income, despite the needs she and her son had. "I couldn't provide for my son the way I wanted to, so I gave to God, believing that He would take care of my son," says Karen. With her family's generous help, she ended up being able to provide far more for Canyon than she could have imagined.

Karen has now been the top national sales person in three different companies. In her current position, her sales performance quickly catapulted her to the top, and she was promoted to manager. She eventually built a sales team in record time, leading it to seize second position in their market.

"God has blessed me so much," recalls Karen with gratitude. "My son just finished law school and is a constant joy to me and others. While I do consider the kind of giving God has called me to do as sacrificial, He always takes care of me. It's become exciting to write the checks and think about those I'm helping!" says Karen with joyful conviction. She adds, "It is such a unique opportunity to be a part of bringing God's people back into Israel—to have a part in the fulfillment of biblical prophecy. For any who have not thought about giving to Israel and the Jewish people, I would tell them, "God specifically says 'I will bless you.' There are no other requirements. This has certainly been true of my experience with Him!"

Ina, Israel

The terrible economic situation and vicious anti-Semitism in the countries of the former Soviet Union lead some Jewish parents to send their children to Israel, where they can hope for a better future.

Ina is one of those children. Now thirteen years old, she still recalls the fear that shadowed her everyday life in Russia. "You can feel the hatred," she shudders. "There are nationalist groups whose members actually kill Jews."

Through *On Wings of Eagles*, Ina was flown to Israel and quickly found a safe home there at *Beit Ulpana*, a boarding school for immigrant girls, funded by *The Fellowship*. There, Ina studies the Torah, and she receives room and board and a small monthly allowance, as well as warmth and guidance.

NEW PRIORITIES

Tedd and Jacki Rhodes, Pennsylvania

TEDD RHODES EXPERIENCED a personal epiphany in his early forties. He and his wife of thirteen years divorced. After years of living on a professional fast track, he made a major career change. As his life took a new and very different course, Tedd was blessed with a friend and partner in his new wife, Jacki. They began a second family together and, today, have four vibrant and gifted children. Completing this family are three older children, all college graduates, all successful and dynamic in their own right.

To his busy family life, Tedd adds lots of wanderlust from his love of road trips and new experiences. "I'm fifty-six now. At this stage in my life, it's all about our children and helping others. I couldn't be happier about my priorities," he says.

Tedd's priorities were largely shaped after viewing *On Wings of Eagles* seven years ago. "When I was a young man, my father once told me the Holocaust was the worst thing that had ever happened in the history of the world," he relays. "That statement stuck with me my entire life."

Pentecostal by denomination, Tedd is an avid student of the Bible. "God wants His people, the Jewish people, to be returned to their homeland. This is part of the plan, and He has asked Christians to be champions of this cause," he says.

Indeed, Tedd has almost a "*Schindler's List*" mentality when it comes to his personal financial choices. "I often wonder how many Jews we could help if we would just re-prioritize our finances. There is probably nothing that we do not have that we really want or need. Jacki and I don't want our lives to be about acquiring things. We want to be about saving and serving people—and having our children understand that this is a lifestyle choice."

Living with such an "others focused" outlook leaves Tedd and Jacki uniquely positioned to hear the voice of God on behalf of those in need. For example, one day a letter arrived from *The Fellowship*, asking for sponsors who would be willing to send $4,200 to refurbish bomb shelters in a hard-hit part of northern Israel. "We try to keep an emergency fund in savings, and providentially, just happened to have $4,200. We immediately looked at each other, laughed, wrote a check, and sent it off. There was no discussion; we both knew right then that we'd had it sitting there for such a time as this."

Tedd and Jacki love to tell how the floodgates of heaven open wide when they give to God's special people through *The Fellowship*. Tedd asserts, "To anyone who has not given, I would say, 'Just try it, and then step back and see what God does in your life.'" After giving to the bomb shelter project, Tedd's sales exploded again, doubling what he and his company had projected. "God consistently puts me at the top of the company in sales. It's not me; it's God. The Jewish people are the apple of His eye, and bringing them back to their homeland is high on His list. It should be on ours, too."

Marat, Israel

A former colonel in the Soviet army, Marat moved with his wife to Israel from the Ukraine, and he has been working as a volunteer with the police department in Shlomi, his adoptive hometown.

When talking about the Second Lebanon War, Marat relates, "I went on a lot of patrols with the police and saw firsthand what all the shelters looked like. Even the best of them weren't fit for use. Most of the people wanted to stay in their apartments rather than go into these shelters. The conditions were so bad that they were willing to take a chance with their lives."

Marat can appreciate more than most the positive impact of *The Fellowship*'s renovations of the shelters. "People are relieved to know that, in the event of another war, they don't have to think twice about going into their shelter."

ay the LORD repay you for what you have done. May you be richly rewarded by the LORD, the God of Israel, under whose wings you have come to take refuge.

RUTH 2:12

he LORD bless you, and keep you; the LORD make His face shine upon you, and be gracious to you; the LORD turn His face toward you, and give you peace.

NUMBERS 6:24-26

International Fellowship of Christians and Jews

LISTENING FOR HIS VOICE

Priscilla Wolfe, Maryland

A WOMAN WHO HAS lived a long, full life, Priscilla Wolfe recently celebrated her eightieth birthday. Andrew, the love of her life, served in World War II as a teenager. Priscilla met him well after the war, and the couple married and began a family in the early 1950s. The Wolfes raised five children on a 123-acre farm in the rural Maryland area.

"We had to walk almost a mile just to get to the road that ran in front of our house," recalls Priscilla with a giggle at the realization of how different things are today for most families. "The whole family helped out with our cows and our small orchard that included cherries, mulberries, peaches, and plums," she adds. "The family canned the fruit and made fresh butter and cottage cheese."

The great-grandchild of a Methodist circuit-riding preacher, Priscilla is quick to point out that "attending church is not the same as having a close relationship with the living God." She adds, "I made my share of mistakes in life, and some carried heavy consequences." As a young mother, Priscilla felt God's presence reaching out to her in a palpable way during a quiet moment at church. She recalls, "I answered through tears, 'Whatever You want from me, I will do it.'" In the twenty years following, her love for God has increased in natural and gratifying ways. She has shown her affection for Him through avid service to others, both as a Sunday school teacher and as a cook for a local kids' church camp. She is praying for good health to cook for one last camp next summer.

Priscilla has had the privilege of visiting Israel twice. God used these trips, along with the scriptures, to ignite her love for the nation and the Jewish people. In particular, she felt a burden for young Jewish girls who were in danger in Iran, and she wanted to help at least one immigrate to Israel.

The opportunity came when Priscilla received a mailing from *The Fellowship*. Thinking it was sent in error, she threw it away. The next day, she received an unexpected check for approximately $300. She remembered the appeal in the mailer and prayed, "But God this is not enough. What do You want me to do?" She sensed that she was to call a friend named Becky and ask her to pray about partnering with her on a donation.

Already a partner of *The Fellowship*, Becky Parsons willingly gave the additional amount that was needed. Both women have encouraged others to be involved in bringing Jews back to Israel—in fact, Becky inspired her preteen Sunday school class to collect enough money to help one Jewish girl make *aliyah*.

"I just want to share how humbled I feel that God chose to speak to me and work through me," recalls Priscilla choking back tears. "When I truly stop to think about it, I realize it's one of the most amazing privileges in this life. I encourage all who love God, to seek Him, listen . . . and then obey. It brings such joy. I've lived a long time to learn that lesson!"

Miriam, Israel

A bright, fifteen-year-old Jewish girl from Ukraine, Miriam was able to escape abject poverty and anti-Semitism in the former Soviet Union when, with help from *The Fellowship*'s *On Wings of Eagles* program, she was sent by her parents to Israel.

Being away from her family has been difficult. But thanks to *Beit Ulpana*, an extraordinary boarding school for new émigré teens, also funded by *The Fellowship*, she now receives three nutritious meals a day, a warm and safe place to live, and a solid, Bible-based education. When the time comes, the school will put her on the road to self-sufficiency by providing job training and counseling. The staff has seen to it that Miriam keeps in close touch with her family in Ukraine. At the same time, she has grown so close to staff members that they are now like a second family to her.

A SPECIAL WAY TO REMEMBER

John & Deborah Harvison, Pennsylvania

ORDAINED MINISTERS IN the Full Gospel tradition since 1984, John and Deborah Harvison have a heart for the poor and oppressed, and especially for suffering Jews around the world. Although not in full-time ministry, John enjoys preaching and serving, and Deborah loves playing the guitar, singing, and speaking to groups as opportunities arise.

John, an electrician for seventeen years, was laid off when his company closed down. He now works as a housekeeper for a nursing home. Deborah, a nurse's aide for sixteen years, was recently placed on full-time disability. True to her spunky spirit, though, she still works part-time as a school crossing guard.

When asked how the Harvisons became involved with *The Fellowship*, Deborah says, "I remember watching a news report a couple of years back and seeing Israel being bombed. It made me mad! I said, 'John, we have to do something.'"

Though their income is truly modest, the Harvisons began by giving ten dollars a month. They were soon able to double that amount. Then, when Deborah's first disability check came in, the couple decided to stretch their faith and commit one hundred dollars a month to the ministry.

John believes it's not the amount that matters most—it's having a giving heart. He says, "A little bit in the hands of God becomes a lot. If everyone would just do a little, it would really make an impact."

On a very personal note, the oldest of the Harvisons' children was stillborn. "Cara Lee Virginia Harvison is thirty-seven now. Can you believe that?" Deborah says with motherly pride. She continues, "We had always wanted to create a monument to Cara Lee, but with our modest income and raising our other children, we never seemed to get around to it. When the day came that we were able to do something, John and I were in total agreement—we both felt the most beautiful way to remember our daughter would be to bring a Jew home in her name."

The Harvisons have already given above their means to *The Fellowship*. However, when contemplating what they would do if they had unlimited time and resources, they didn't hesitate to say, "With God as our witness, it would be to bring as many Jews home as we could."

Sagu, Israel

At age fifty, Ethiopian native Sagu realized his dream of coming to Israel. "My father and grandfather never saw their dream come true, but their spirit is alive inside me," says Sagu. "I am sure they know we made it to the Promised Land."

Thanks to *The Fellowship*'s *On Wings of Eagles* program, Sagu and his two teenage sons made *aliyah*. Their arrival in Israel was bittersweet, however, as Sagu's wife died of a heart attack just before they made the trip.

Shortly after arriving in Israel, his lifelong struggle with diabetes caused him to go blind. But before his sight darkened completely, he had his sons take him to as many places as possible in Jerusalem, including the Western Wall. "These are my final images from this lifetime. They will sustain me until my last day," he says with heartfelt emotion. "Thanks to God, I feel like a king. Living in Israel is the biggest blessing anyone can have."

RIDING HIGH

Kathy Sullivan, South Carolina

KATHY SULLIVAN WAS a city girl who always longed to be a country girl—that's because she had a deep affinity for animals, horses in particular. At seven years old, Kathy knew she wanted to ride and compete in horse shows. When she was twelve, she actually bought a horse "on credit" without her parents' knowledge. "I cleaned house and made meals for pay," recalls Kathy, "and I made payments on my horse. Of course, my parents found out about it after a while!"

Just out of high school, Kathy had the opportunity to take a different kind of ride—one that took her feet a lot higher off the ground than a horse could. "A friend of mine had his pilot's license, and he took me up for a ride. I remember thinking, 'This is what

I want to do for a living. If *he* can do it, I sure can!'"

Kathy was naturally gifted at aeronautics and related studies. In college, she majored in business and minored in aeronautical science. After graduation, she worked for commuter airlines and eventually reached her dream of becoming a commercial pilot (at a time when this was very rare for a woman). She's been flying commercially now for twenty-three years. She also still pursues her passion for flying on the back of a horse, for she shows champion cutting horses in competition.

Though she's not afraid to pilot a plane, Kathy has had to battle fear at times, especially when God's prompted her to reach out to strangers. However, as a woman who "doesn't quit easily," she's fought through those fears. Today, she holds treasured memories of divine encounters where she shared God's love and grace. On one such occasion at a horse show, Kathy felt impressed to give a Bible and some scriptures to a total stranger. Upon receiving the Bible, the woman began to cry. She said, "I had been praying for God to show me He was real."

Kathy found out later that this woman was a national leader in the business world. "It was so humbling. I couldn't believe God used me in that way, and I'm sad to think

I almost blew it out of fear," relays Kathy. "I've learned that God will use anyone who is willing and that the more we believe Him, the more He demonstrates His power."

As she grew in her faith, Kathy found herself falling in love with the Old Testament. "I became aware, simply by reading the Bible, that Israel was God's land and the Jews were His people," she recalls. "I was astonished at how many educated people don't read or study the Bible. In my view, this has contributed to widespread ignorance regarding the need to stand for Israel."

An avid *Fellowship* supporter and a firm believer that Christians should "show" their love to others, Kathy relates, "I want the Jewish people to know that I care and that my care translates into action. I am typically reluctant to be public in any way about my personal giving—whether service or finances. But if my passion for the Jews ignites something in another person who's perhaps been unaware or 'on the fence,' then I'm willing to share my testimony."

Paul, Ukraine

Fifteen-year-old old Paul lives with his family in the Ukraine in a two-room house. In winter, their only heat comes from a small kitchen stove.

When Paul was young, he was severely injured in a car accident, and after that trauma, he suffered mental disabilities and eventually stopped speaking. In addition to this sorrow, the family had to survive on Paul's disability stipend, a meager $50 per month.

Fortunately, the local *Hesed* center, funded by *The Fellowship*'s *Isaiah 58* program, sent Paul to a speech therapist and a psychologist twice a week, and he has begun to speak again.

"We did not think it was possible," said Paul's mother. "But, thank God, my boy has changed!"

International Fellowship of Christians and Jews

A BISHOP WHO STANDS FOR ISRAEL

Jason Sanderson, New Hampshire

A BISHOP WITH THE Liberal Catholic Church International, Jason Sanderson is a man with a huge heart and many talents. Displaying a quick wit and hearty laugh, he also is a man at ease with himself and others.

Jason was born the youngest of six children, thirteen years after the birth of his nearest sibling. It's no wonder then, that Jason experienced an upbringing similar to that of an only child. Jason's family was impacted by alcoholism, which influenced him to seek monastery training right after high school graduation. He recalls, "I wanted to get as far away from Vermont as I could, and I ended up in Texas!"

Jason spent nine years in monastery, becoming an ordained priest along the way.

Today, he oversees two parishes, in New Hampshire and Maine, respectively. He is also his denomination's bishop for the continent of Africa. The scope of outreach there involves nineteen missions, six orphanages, two schools, one clinic, one women's program, five priests, and five deacons. "Whew!" says Jason of the list of duties. "But this is what I love to do, and it comes naturally to me."

Interestingly, he also had a career as a professional wrestler. "In those days, the lines were clearly drawn," he says dramatically. "It was more of a morality play between good and evil, and you knew the good guy would win." A single father of two young sons, Jason decided to end his career when the sport took an ominous turn toward steroids use. Even so, he still attends a yearly wrestling convention that includes giving a humanitarian award, of which he has been a past, albeit reluctant, recipient.

A caring man by nature, Jason recalls, "I always had great regard for the Jewish people. I had a dear friend in high school who was Jewish." But it wasn't until later, while studying for the priesthood and delving into theology and church history, that he realized how Christianity is "rooted" in Judaism.

"The whole biblical connection between the Jewish people and God's plan for them in the world just really struck me hard." During the Afghanistan War, the events in Iraq, and 9/11, God laid a burden to pray for Israel on the bishop's heart. He says, "I became more aware of the rise of anti-Semitism around the world and vowed that when I was able, I would do more for these people."

Bishop Sanderson has since been "doing more" through his involvement with *The Fellowship*. "I would strongly urge anyone to help with the financial needs of God's chosen people. When a person gives, no matter the amount, the mere act of giving becomes a tangible connection with the Jewish people," he says.

Jason participated in a *Fellowship* shelter project. At first, due to his "anonymous giving" policy, he was hesitant to have his name inscribed on the shelter. "Then later," he recalls with passion, "I thought, 'Why not?' Now I actually like the idea of having the words *Bishop Jason Sanderson* written there. That way, the Jewish people can see, no matter what's happened in the past, there's a bishop in America who stands for Israel." He teasingly adds, "I've even envisioned my wrestling photo on the door, facing enemy territory, to help make the children feel a little safer!"

Mark, Israel

During the Second Lebanon War, Mark moved with his wife from the Ukraine to northern Israel. In describing their building's bomb shelter, he says, "It was full of bugs and broken glass, with no beds or running water. You didn't want to go in, and once in, you couldn't wait to get out."

Thanks to *The Fellowship*'s substantial donations to renovate Israeli shelters, Mark and his wife won't have to face these conditions again. He says, "It's hard to believe this is the same shelter that I so dreaded going into during the war. It's brand new, and it has everything a person needs in an emergency. It's heartwarming to know that we're not alone. I hope we'll never need the shelters, but we feel much safer knowing that they're here for our protection."

lessed is he who has regard for the weak; the LORD delivers him in times of trouble. The LORD will protect him and preserve his life; he will bless him in the land.

PSALM 41:1-2

e who is kind to the poor lends to the LORD, and he

will reward him for what he has done.

PROVERBS 19:17

International Fellowship of Christians and Jews

LEAP OF FAITH

Mike and Kenna Day, South Carolina

IT'S BEEN A long and winding road, both spiritually and personally, for Mike and Kenna Day, owners of a successful furniture business in Greenville, South Carolina. But like many other entrepreneurs, they have endured plenty of hardship along the path to becoming profitable.

"Mike and I grew up in a small town called Easley, not far from Greenville, so we've known each other for a very long time," recalls Kenna. "Neither of us was raised attending church, although we had good families. "It was the sixties," Mike says, "and I was a bit of a rebel anyway. The love of my life at that time was my music. I played guitar and percussion, and sang at bars."

Nonetheless, when Mike was twenty, God touched his heart and turned his life completely around. Kenna reminisces, "The change was so dramatic—from how he looked and talked to how he lived—that his conversion had a tremendous influence in my coming to faith . . . life-changing, *personal* faith."

Although the couple was blessed with good health and loving children, they struggled to obtain a steady income that would allow them to be the generous givers they longed to become. "For many years," recalls Mike, "we lived from paycheck to paycheck and drove a clunker of a car. At one point, we were even on the verge of losing our home. We just couldn't seem to rise above a certain financial level."

At that time, the Days were making about $500 per week. One night, they were surfing through TV channels looking for some good preaching, when they came across Rabbi Eckstein asking Christians to bring Jewish exiles back home to Israel. They immediately decided to act upon the invitation. "Our first goal was to send one Jew home per month," Mike says. "We felt honored and blessed to be able to maintain that level for about a year."

Then, as can so often happen for the self-employed, their finances took a downward turn. Kenna recalls, "That was a critical point in our fledgling business. So I walked over to a mirror in our modest showroom and prayed, 'Lord, why have we been allowed to look like the tail when your Word says we are the head? We are your children. I have faith that your Word will manifest in our lives, because your Word will never fail!'"

The very next day, a woman walked into the store and ordered enough furniture for eighteen resort-style rental condominium properties in Florida. Her order far exceeded what their showroom could even hold. Their previous goal of sending one Jew home per month turned into twenty sent home in a single month, just from that sale alone.

"It felt so wonderful to be able to give," says Kenna. "The windows of heaven opened, and God's blessings started pouring out upon us abundantly. Our sales increased from bankrupt status to over $1 million per year!" Mike adds, "Our lives and financial situation have far exceeded what we could have imagined ten years ago. It all came together at the same time we began giving to God's people, the Jews—and it has not let up!"

Bogeh, Israel

Bogeh, a blind, thirty-two-year-old Ethiopian Jew, has faced many challenges in his life, including the death of his mother when he was only four years old. It wasn't until he was a young adult that he had the opportunity to learn Braille and study Judaism.

With his father and two brothers, Bogeh came to Israel as part of *The Fellowship's On Wings of Eagles* program. "It was the culmination of a dream," he says joyfully.

Bogeh is counting on a bright future in Israel. Already, his Jewish identity and faith in God have deepened. "In Israel, I learn Hebrew in the morning and listen to Hebrew Torah tapes all afternoon," he says. "I go to prayers three times a day, and for the first time in my life, I feel like a welcome member of the community."

International Fellowship of Christians and Jews

WE CAME TO LOVE THEM THROUGH THE BIBLE

Bruce and Lavetta Pope, Minnesota

A LIVELY, UPBEAT COUPLE, Bruce and Lavetta Pope love sharing life together and serving those in need. Bruce has held the career positions of contractor, nursing home administrator, and pastor, which has been perhaps his favorite. Lavetta has enjoyed a profession as a nurse working with chemically dependent patients. She finds her work extraordinarily rewarding.

Now in his seventies, Bruce speaks with exuberance when retelling stories of helping people find God. In one memorable account, he relates the journey of a prisoner who had shot his own mother. The young man was so full of remorse that he spoke with Bruce at length about the burning question, "How can I ever be right with God?" Pastor Bruce counseled and prayed with this man who was bound up in pain. Later, Bruce learned that the prisoner had received a vision of his mother, joyful in heaven, and was able to receive forgiveness and a new beginning.

The Popes wholeheartedly believe that serving others must extend beyond one's immediate circle. For example, they have an undeniable bond with their Jewish brothers and sisters. "We came to love them through the Bible," recalls Bruce. "I consider myself like Abraham—in a brotherhood of believers with the Jews. As Christians, we *must* help them."

This service-oriented duo had followed Rabbi Eckstein for "quite some years" on television. But one Saturday evening, Bruce experienced an unusual occurrence that forever changed his mindset on giving. As he sat down near the television, he noticed the remote control nearby, pointed away from the screen. All at once, the television turned on by itself—Bruce never touched the remote. In recounting the story, he asserts, "There was Rabbi Eckstein presenting *On Wings of Eagles*. I was so moved. Then, as I continued watching, I felt the Holy Spirit say to me, 'Give ten thousand dollars.'".

Bruce struggled for a few days with this heavenly directive. He and Lavetta did not have much discretionary income. "I wanted to be prepared for any emergencies that might arise as we were getting older," he relays. Even so, after much prayer and confirmation, Bruce sent the money to *The Fellowship*.

How did Lavetta respond? Bruce laughs, and quips, "Well, she hasn't clobbered me yet!" Then he quickly adds, "Seriously, she supported me in this decision. She always does in these matters."

This joyful, loving couple encourages anyone who is considering giving to *The Fellowship* to "pray and listen to the voice of God." Bruce adds, "Only God could have compelled us to do what we did. We know from experience that He guides those who are truly seeking His will and plan for their lives."

Rivka, Israel

Rivka and her family felt greatly blessed to be in the Holy Land, but the transition from rural Ethiopia to modern Israel was especially challenging for the Ethiopian immigrants. Israel's economic problems meant Rivka's father couldn't find regular work, especially since he did not speak Hebrew.

The family continued in poverty. Still, Rivka worked hard in school. She dreamed of studying the Torah and becoming a doctor. But how?

Rivka's parents learned of a program for immigrant children, funded by *The Fellowship's On Wings of Eagles*. Through this program, she receives help preparing for college.

Says Riva with deep gratitude, "Perhaps, through my future service to the people of Israel, I'll be able to repay all that I've received."

International Fellowship of Christians and Jews

A FRIEND FOR LIFE

Irina Azar, California

IRINA AZAR WAS born in a refugee camp in the southern part of Germany. "I remember, from my earliest days, that we had a 'Zion box' on our wall. It was a small blue box with a Star of David on it. Being poor refugees, we had very little money. Even so, whenever my father had an extra penny or two, we would have a little ceremony and put the money in the box to help the Jewish people," she recounts.

As a young girl in Berlin, and during Hitler's ascent to power, Irina was able to get admitted to school on a scholarship. While there, she became friends with a girl named Charlotte, or Lottie, as everyone called her. "I didn't know she was Jewish. She was simply my friend," she says.

"My father often told me, 'Live by the truth and God will rescue you,'" relays Irina with conviction, adding "I've put a lot of thought into why I've always loved the Jewish people. I'm sure it started with my father's love for 'God's children.' I remember him taking me on his knee and telling me that we were to bless them. He didn't just say it—he believed we ought to act on our faith as well."

One day the new school director (who had been appointed by the Nazis) looked out his window and saw Irina speaking to Lottie. The Director called Irina into his office and forbade her to speak with Lottie or any other Jew again.

"I refused," says Irina, "and because I did not follow his instruction, I began having great difficulties in school. It seemed that everything I did was scrutinized and found to be unsatisfactory. Nevertheless, I would not give up my Jewish friend." The words of Irina's father rang in her ears, "When you are a friend, you are a friend for life."

"This is how I feel about the Jewish people," says Irina emphatically, "That is my commitment. I pray for the Jewish people morning and night. I have a *Mezuzah* on my front door and another at my back door. I never leave without praying that God will bless and keep them from the dangers that surround them."

Irina immigrated to the United States in 1949. She later moved to San Francisco where she attended university and made a close friend there, a Jewish woman named Lilly. When Irina's husband of twenty-two years walked out on her, she became isolated and depressed. One day she happened to spot Lilly across a busy street, "Irina!" she called out, and they embraced. "It was the first time in so long that I felt loved. We picked up our relationship again and became a support to one another." Lilly's friendship was a beautiful reward for Irena's commitment to Lottie and other Jewish people.

On the trip she took to Israel with *The Fellowship*, Irina felt nothing but love wherever she went. She was especially touched by the children's homes and other outreaches to those in need. "Ten years ago. I began giving to *The Fellowship*," says Irina. "I have found that the more I understand, the more I am motivated to give. If we call ourselves Christians, we must show love and compassion for what the Jewish people have endured, and continue to endure."

. . .

Irina passed away on December 16, 2008. She will be deeply misssed by the many lives she has lovingly touched.

Alem, Israel

Alem, a young Ethiopian woman, made *aliyah* with her mother and three siblings. At first, Alem's mother cleaned houses to support the family, while her older brother worked in a factory. But then Alem's mother became ill and her brother was disabled in a work accident. Alem worked day and night caring for them, and tried to keep up her schoolwork. But soon, her own health began to fail—the strain was too much.

A social worker told the family about ELEM, a ministry of *The Fellowship's Guardians of Israel*. The organization arranged disability pensions for Alem's mother and brother, and paid for household help a few times a week.

The Fellowship's partners saved this family from ruin, and gave Alem the chance to ensure her future by enabling her to focus on her studies.

International Fellowship of Christians and Jews

LIKE FATHER, LIKE SON

Robert Fulton, North Carolina

ROBERT FULTON IS a man of deep conviction, especially when it comes to his work ethic and "going out on a limb" to give to people in real need. He is gentle, with a lilting southern accent, yet strong and direct regarding the principles that anchor his life and faith.

A construction worker, Robert works long, grueling hours in water systems and sewer-related construction—a business he and his brother literally built with the sweat of their backs over twenty years. "We often work sun up to sun down, but I sure sleep well! I even went nine years once without taking vacation," cites Robert, as if he would prefer not to do *that* again.

The brothers each take a modest salary, and Robert is extremely conservative financially, always prepared for the occasional, inevitable economic downturn.

One day, a friend told Robert that in a third-world country, a church could be built for as little as $1,500! This amazing reality stuck in Robert's mind. He could not escape it.

Back at home, Robert and his wife, Vicki, were remodeling their home. "We were up to our ears in debt," Robert divulges with a note of sadness. "Finally, I got up the nerve to tell Vicki that we were going to 'build a church.' Her eyes got really big. We didn't have the money, and she wasn't exactly sure what I meant!"

Feeling led to take out a loan to "buy a church," Robert donated the money and was able to pay it back within a year. To build more churches, he took out a second loan for twice as much the following year, and also paid that back within a year.

Then, a few years ago, Robert heard about *The Fellowship*. "I had my hand in so many pies, that I was concerned about overextending myself." Nonetheless, this strong man with a tender heart could not escape the burning desire to bring Russian Jews home. And that's exactly what he did. Twenty-eight Jews came home—thanks to the generous $10,000 gift from a portion of Robert's hard-earned retirement fund, complete with added penalties and taxes.

Much later, this father of a preteen felt it was important for his twelve-year-old son, Robert Daniel, to see *On Wings of Eagles*. They sat down together and watched it. Afterward, Robert said, "Son, I just want you to think about what you've seen for a while. We'll talk about it again sometime."

Not long afterward, Robert Daniel had the opportunity to make some money at a local fair by running the family "trackless train" ride and selling kettle corn. That particular fair brought in a whopping $700 for a very happy twelve-year-old.

The next day, as the two Roberts were shooting hoops together, the elder Robert inquired, "Hey, son! What are you going to do with all that money?" He winked with pride at the budding businessman but was totally unprepared for the answer that shot back at him.

Without hesitation, Robert Daniel replied, "Dad, I want to give it all to *On Wings of Eagles*."

Today, even in retelling the story, Dad Fulton stills gets choked up with tears of pride and joy. What a beautiful heritage of faith and giving Robert is sharing with his son!

Andre, Israel

During the dark days of communism, many Jews in the former Soviet Union kept their religion a secret. Parents often concealed their Jewish faith from their own children. Andre was one of those children. But at the death of his grandmother, his mother chose a Jewish cemetery for her. "What a surprise it was!" Andre remarked.

As Andre got older and grew in his faith, he knew that his own children had no future in Russia. Communism had fallen, but anti-Semitism and poverty still plagued the country.

Andre longed to bring his family to Israel but couldn't afford it. Thankfully, they were flown to the Holy Land by *The Fellowship*'s *On Wings of Eagles*. At home in Jerusalem, they're elated to be learning Hebrew and receiving job training.

peak up for those who cannot speak for themselves, for

the rights of all who are destitute. Speak up and judge fairly;

defend the rights of the poor and needy.

PROVERBS 31:8-9

will bless those who bless you, and whosoever curses you I will curse; and all peoples on earth will be blessed through you.

GENESIS 12:3

International Fellowship of Christians and Jews

PROVIDENCE AT EVERY TURN

Barbara Walker, South Dakota

A WOMAN OF MANY interests, Barbara Walker held various jobs throughout her life—from hotel maid, to nursing home aide, to teacher. Her seven years working with children in a bookmobile setting fueled her desire to get her teaching degree and a Masters degree.

Having always been drawn to music, Barbara especially enjoys the rhythms, sounds, and dancing of the Jewish culture. "I remember in 1998, I was a single mother with a preteen son when I heard about a fifty-year jubilee being planned for the State of Israel in Orlando, Florida," she recalls. "There would be dancing and singing and music, and I could just envision myself there. Yet I felt I could not afford to go."

This woman of faith decided to pray about the deep desire in her heart. Within a short time, she sensed God telling her, "You are going!" She made it to Florida, and the event turned out to be one of the most memorable times of her life. "I can still remember people lifting up prayer shawls and the sound of shofars, all mixed in with the aroma of anointing oil. It was rapturous!"

Toward the end of the conference, Barbara and a few friends had given most of their money to Jewish-oriented ministries. "But God provided!" remembers Barbara, the magnitude of His provision still fresh to her to this day. "We took a certain amount of money out of our hotel room, but after giving most of it to ministries, we didn't check to see if we would be covered for dinner. My friends and I barely had enough to pay for our meal and tip, when, for no apparent reason, the restaurant manager announced that the meal was free. We were stunned."

On a cab ride the next day, the friends were surprised when the driver inquired about the conference, asking them to pray for him. Still amazed at the divine appointment, Barbara recalls, "When we reached our destination, he said, 'There's no charge—I can't charge passengers who prayed for me so beautifully!'"

Later, Barbara and her friends learned of a special anniversary trip to Israel. How she longed to go! But financially, it was a big stretch. In any case, Barbara decided to read the brochure and pray over it, to "see what God might do." Shortly thereafter, she received word that she was going to be awarded a large sum from a long-pending case. Upon hearing the news, a close friend burst out, "Barbara . . . you can go now!"

A student of prophecy and a fan of Christian leaders who emphasize the importance of Jewish customs, traditions, and holidays, Barbara's faith has deepened through her connection with the Jewish people. "Rabbi Eckstein has also been a great inspiration to me. When I saw all those elderly Jews living in poverty in Russia on the television broadcast, it just broke my heart. I had to give," she says. "These people are God's chosen ones. When we give to them, we partake in a covenant promise of blessing."

Fira, Russia

An elderly Russian Jew, Fira has lived a life of great hardship. As a child, she was forced to flee her village because of the *pogroms*, so common in the region during the early 1900s. During World War II, the family had to run away from the German army.

After the war, Fira married, and for a time things were better. But later, her husband deserted her. Today, Fira lives alone in a one-bedroom apartment in Moscow. Now elderly, she suffers from numerous medical problems.

Fira is now being helped through *Chama*, an organization supported by *The Fellowship*'s *Isaiah 58* program. Through *Chama*, Fira receives food and medication. "I'm so happy somebody cares about me," she smiles.

International Fellowship of Christians and Jews

INFLUENCING MINDS AND HEARTS

Beth and Arthur McInnis, Texas

LIFELONG PARTNERS IN marriage and ministry, Arthur and Beth McInnis are a power-packed couple, specializing in what "love in action" can do. Beth, a mother of three, with a passion for kids and education, went back to school in her forties to earn her teaching degree. She now teaches in a small rural high school in Texas. Her husband, Arthur, an ordained minister, self-described as "unconventional," has had careers as a pastor, tax appraiser, and "a few others in between," he says with a chuckle.

"I was so proud of Beth when she went back to school and pursued her passion," says Arthur. "She's an amazing teacher." Indeed, Beth is a real go-getter who digs deep into the subjects she teaches, including a unit on the Holocaust.

"When I went back to school, I was deeply affected by a book entitled *Ordinary Men*, a collection of memoirs by men who carried out many of Hitler's orders. I bawled my eyes out reading it." Since that time, Beth has immersed herself in the history of the Jewish people, specifically the Holocaust. It is her mission to influence the minds and hearts of her students concerning anti-Semitism and other forms of racial hatred.

On two separate occasions, Beth was chosen to represent her school district at a national Holocaust conference. She credits the first conference as being the most life-changing event she has ever experienced, besides her coming to faith.

Over a year ago, the McInnises came across a letter from *The Fellowship*. "We couldn't believe that Holocaust survivors who'd already gone through so much were now in need of basic things like food, clothing, and shelter!" The couple became partners with the ministry. "We can't even begin to describe the blessings that have been bestowed upon us since we've begun giving," relays Beth. Giving has become a family affair now, with Beth's parents and her older son joining in the cause.

"God has not forgotten His people," relays Arthur. "Jesus was a Jew. The Christian faith has many roots in Judaism. The more Christians study the traditions and culture of the Jewish faith, the more deeply they can understand their own faith. I love the Jews. God loves the Jews and has a special plan for them. Our part is to love and support His chosen people."

The McInnis family keeps contact with a Jewish restaurant owner in their small Texas town. Says Beth, "He was one of the 'hidden children'—kept safe by Catholic nuns who had his name changed. I would love to know more, but we understand that the subject of those horrible times can be very painful for someone to talk about. Someday, our dream is to pray at the Wailing Wall. And, of course, because of my passion to keep the memory of the Holocaust in view, I would like to visit Europe." Arthur adds, "If people took the time to get to know and understand other people and cultures, I'm convinced there would be less racial discrimination. It broke our hearts when we saw the elderly Jews in Russia suffering. We are blessed beyond measure to have some part in alleviating some of that pain."

Sasha, Israel

Sasha, a Russian Jew who was abandoned by his parents, spent his childhood in numerous orphanages, where he performed poorly in school, got into fights, and had no friends.

Then Sasha got the chance to live in Israel. After enrolling in a boarding school funded by *The Fellowship*, he learned discipline and guidance, and showed potential and intelligence. He completed college entrance exams and entered pre-military training, aiming to become a naval officer.

Now eighteen years old, Sasha says, "*Guardians of Israel* has changed my life. I'm much more mature now. I give much thanks to the people who donate to *The Fellowship*."

International Fellowship of Christians and Jews

GIVING FROM A FULL HEART

Evelyn Betita, California

EVELYN BETITA IS a determined and kind-hearted woman of Philippine and Chinese heritage. She has spent most of her adult life in California, where she and her beloved husband raised their four children and have enjoyed the close companionship of ten delightful grandchildren.

Now seventy-five years old and widowed, Evelyn's voice sounds like that of a much younger woman. Her spirit is at once kind and strong. Hard work has been a way of life for Evelyn, who seems to take much pride, and even *joy*, in her legacy of service to corporations and her fellow man.

"I spent sixteen years working as a record inspector for CBS Records," recalls Evelyn with the slight halting hint of an accent. "When the company moved, I worked for a microchip company for almost ten years." She is thankful for God's provision of work for her family during those years.

After her previous careers ended, and even though advanced in years herself, she became a caregiver for the elderly. "I am so glad to have my work so that I can help God's people through *The Fellowship*," says a spirited Evelyn. She then adds, "I don't have much, but I give as much as I can!"

Evelyn reflects on seeing a presentation of *On Wings of Eagles*: "When I saw the elderly Jews' living conditions—no heat, food, or medicine—I cried. I felt so sorry in my heart. I had to help. I have also been influenced by several pastors and some of our nation's policy makers to help the Jewish people. I bless God's people every day," says Evelyn. "I don't know how to thank God enough for this opportunity to help bring His people back to Israel. I want to obey God, but I give because I love them, too!"

Recently, Evelyn was speaking with a gardener friend, telling him of God's special people and His promises to those who bless them. The gardener replied, "Well, I guess I should do that too!" Evelyn made sure he was introduced to the ministry of

The Fellowship. "God has blessed me so much. I have such good health and am still strong enough to work as a caregiver to a woman who has Alzheimer's. My children are well, although one daughter has Lupus—but I believe God answers our prayers and that He will take care of her."

Ever the hard worker and big-hearted giver, Evelyn's newest goal (at the young age of seventy-five!) is to open a care home with her grown granddaughters. She asks, "Please pray that we can achieve this goal so that we can give more to the ministry. What *The Fellowship* is doing is fulfillment of prophecy—for God to gather His people back together in their homeland. I pray that many people will be touched to give and to pray for Israel every day and night."

Ovadiah, Israel

Ovadiah grew up as a member of the *Bnei Menashe*, descendants of one of Israel's "lost tribes" living in India. His parents raised him well in his Jewish faith. But living in Israel was only a cherished dream.

In his forties, Ovadiah learned that the *Bnei Menashe* could return to Israel through *The Fellowship*'s *On Wings of Eagles* program. He could hardly believe it! He was blessed to travel with fifty-one other members of his group. They sang and celebrated the entire trip.

In Israel, the group went to an absorption center where they're learning Hebrew and meeting other Jewish immigrants. Ovadiah and his friends were given the opportunity for a new life in Israel—fulfilling the biblical promise of gathering its exiles "from the four corners of the earth!"

International Fellowship of Christians and Jews

PUTTING CONVICTION INTO ACTION

Troy & Elisa Blaylock, Alaska

TROY AND ELISA Blaylock make their home in Anchorage, Alaska, a notable contrast from the scenery of places where Troy lived during his twenty-year career in the air force. As one might expect, Troy is a man of conviction and action. He also is a man with a tender heart toward God's chosen people.

"I served in Vietnam, mostly as a superintendent with a specialty in administration," relays the seasoned veteran. A committed serviceman who has seen the horrors of war up close, Troy took on other tasks during his service, as well. "I did whatever was needed to get the job done," the patriot relays, the resolve to protect his country evident in his voice.

Now seventy-four, Troy exhibits the same resolve to "get the job done" when it comes to helping feed, clothe, and move Jewish immigrants out of deplorable conditions—whether they live in anti-Semitic countries or on the streets of Israel.

"I was raised in the Pentecostal, Assemblies of God tradition," says Troy, a serious student of Middle Eastern events as they relate to the Bible. "Many people don't realize that Iraq, where my son now serves in the military, is the area where Abraham came from. The Garden of Eden is also in that area, near the Tigris and Euphrates Rivers. And the ruins of the city of Nineveh, where Jonah ministered, are in the mountains there," he asserts. "Every book in the Bible was written by a Jew—even the Gospels! Christians have such a deep connection to God's chosen people."

Like many other *Fellowship* donors, Troy and Elisa live on a fixed income. Still, Troy says with great sincerity, "Oh, I'm not done giving to the Jews. Whenever we have extra money, God's chosen people are at the top of our list to share our blessing. I recently told God I would dedicate our tax return to the Jewish people, and wouldn't you know it? The refund was larger than I expected!" Troy believes with all his heart that God looks after not only the Jewish people, but also those who help them.

"Elisa and I encourage those who have not been aware of God's call to be a blessing to Israel, to take His mandate seriously and become involved—even if they think their contribution is small," says Troy. He firmly believes that Christians, no matter their age, denomination, or financial background, can do great things together because they worship a mighty God.

Doron & Motti, Israel

Several years ago, two young brothers, Doron and Motti, experienced a devastating loss when their mother abandoned the family. The boys now live in the Israeli city of Yoqne'am with their father. He is a caring man who, in order to provide for them, holds several jobs and spends much time away from home. Until recently, Doron and Motti often spent hours wandering the streets after school, a constant worry to their father.

One day a social worker invited the boys to attend *HaPina Shelanu*, a *Fellowship*-sponsored "afternoon center" for needy children. Now, the boys engage in constructive activities, participate in sports, and receive counseling to help them heal from the loss of their mother. Their gratitude to *The Fellowship*'s *Guardians of Israel* is reflected in their bright smiles as they leave the center at the end of each visit.

ow beautiful on the mountains are the feet of those who

bring good news, who proclaim peace, who bring good tidings,

who proclaim salvation, who say to Zion, "Your God reigns!"

ISAIAH 52:7

he fruit of righteousness will be peace; the effect of righteousness will be quietness and confidence forever. My people will live in peaceful dwelling places, in secure homes, in undisturbed places of rest.

ISAIAH 32:17-18

International Fellowship of Christians and Jews

A SPECIAL BOND

John & Sheila Rollow, Colorado

A NATURAL CONVERSATIONALIST WHO engages others easily with her kind heart and quick laughter, Sheila Rollow is a devoted mother of two grown daughters and loving life-partner with husband John. Sheila recalls with a hint of romantic nostalgia, "God has blessed this union of a Baptist girl and Catholic boy for over forty years." Now in their sixties, the Rollows remain ever watchful for God's leading—believing something "new" may be on the horizon for their family, which they describe as "unconventional," citing a penchant for creativity and adventure.

The Rollows shared the military life via a career that has spanned thirty years, including John's service tour in Vietnam. Later, the young captain attended dental school at

Case Western Reserve in Ohio while still serving in the military. Almost 90 percent of his classmates were Jewish. Sheila and John lived in a Jewish community and "got along fabulously" with their new neighbors. Sheila says, "We were immersed in the culture, food, music, and most importantly, friendships—we loved it all!"

Though Sheila had earned a degree with an emphasis in marketing, she developed a keen interest in interior design. "My Jewish neighbor Carrie was instrumental in helping me find my first class to attend," she relays. "My first design job was working for a Jewish woman named Mrs. Hertzmark. She taught me much." The Rollows' insurance broker was also Jewish. They credit his influence as pivotal in enabling John to open his first dental practice.

During the 1980s, John was promoted to commander. Sheila set aside her interior design career for a life of service to the wives and families under her husband's command. In 1987, before the demise of the Berlin Wall, she had the opportunity to travel to East Berlin and Prague with other military wives. Once there, she was astonished at the pervasive poverty and sense of hopelessness in the eyes of the people.

A few years after the trip, God began impressing upon Sheila the desire to be more involved in giving to His work throughout the world. "One day while flipping through the channels, I happened to see *On Wings of Eagles*," Sheila says. "I felt compelled to give after seeing firsthand the desolation of some of these communist-ruled cities. I knew we had to do something to help get these people back to Israel." John readily agreed, and the couple began giving. Their giving, like their heart for God's people, has continued to grow over time.

Sheila has had the opportunity to travel to Israel on several occasions. She recalls with warm reverence, "Whenever I step on the soil of the Holy Land, it feels different from any other place on earth. When I lay my hands and head on the Wailing Wall, every time, tears just pour down my face. The presence of God is palpable."

John and Sheila Rollow have never wavered from their Christian faith, even in the face of life's many challenges. They remain faithful prayer warriors who pray for the peace of Israel and their Jewish friends daily—and encourage others to do the same!

Vadim, Israel

For Vadim and his family, being Jews in the former Soviet Union meant dealing with anti-Semitism on a daily basis, not to mention serious poverty. Vadim worked as a welder, but wages were so low the family could barely manage to live.

One day, they discovered *On Wings of Eagles*. With great joy, the family learned they would be flown to Israel—even though it was a dangerous time when Israel's enemies were firing rockets daily into the country.

"We were scared," Vadim said, "but we had faith that everything would be all right." And it is. *The Fellowship* placed the family in an absorption center in Jerusalem, away from the fighting, where they began Hebrew language studies. Vadim will also receive help in finding construction work.

International Fellowship of Christians and Jews

A HEART FOR GIVING

Dianne Kessler-Bosak, Ohio

DIANNE KESSLER GREW up in the South in extreme poverty, enduring much personal hardship. The oldest of six children, she cared for her younger siblings because her mother was often ill and away from home. At times, the children collected soda bottles to scrape up enough cash to share a small amount of candy—their only sustenance of the day.

"It's okay," Dianne reassures. A caring adult with a ready laugh and quick wit, she says, "Life was hard back then, but God has filled me with love instead of bitterness."

As the story goes, when Dianne was making her bed one day, God touched her heart in a profound way. She remembers the distinct moment when He made His presence known:

"I simply fell in love. I felt that what God wanted most from me was to love Him."

Not long after that experience, Dianne says God laid it on her heart to do something special for Him. "I had seen *On Wings of Eagles*, and I prayed, 'God, if it's all right with You, we could really use some help financially, because I would love to bring Jews back to the Promised Land.'"

God answered her request soon afterward. While helping her husband, Greg, with their locksmith business, Dianne met a special customer. She recounts, "Clara was a sweet, elderly woman. She kept locking herself out of her house, and I just never had the heart to charge her." Over time the two women became friends.

One day Clara said to Dianne, "I'm moving, and I need to sell my house. I really want you to buy it." Dianne offered to take a look at the modest home but assured Clara that she and Greg could not afford it. Even after they'd looked at the property and knew they could work on it and sell it for a profit, Dianne and Greg still weren't convinced they could secure a loan.

But Clara remained determined. "I really want you to buy my house!" she insisted. As it turns out, her resolve encouraged the couple to piece together a loan and purchase the home. "I was thrilled," recalls Dianne. "I knew God had made it all possible."

With much of the profit from their investment, Dianne was able to send approximately thirty Jews home. "I was captivated," she says. "I couldn't wait to do more. I wanted to send at least one Jew home a month."

Dianne kept her old car running well for several years, saving each car payment to put toward her dream—that is, until the car became irreparable. "I was so discouraged. I wanted to keep sending Jews back to Israel." Then, in an unexpected turn of events, a family member called Dianne and offered to buy her a brand new car!

"Oh! The stories I could tell you," relays Dianne. "I have had miracles and seen visions, including an angelic being who appeared when my infant grandson died suddenly." She adds, "Some people think I'm crazy. But I don't care. I know I've seen the hand of God move in my life."

"The Jews are my spiritual brothers and sisters," she adds. "I am a part of them! How could I, someone who has known much suffering, not reach out to God's family in need?"

Eugene, Israel

As Holocaust survivors, Eugene's parents purposefully taught him about their tragic experience. Sadly, anti-Semitism was still alive and well in Russia, where the family lived. "In public school, I was the only Jewish student," he says. "Every time I got less than an 'A' my teacher told me I was stupid because I was Jewish."

Eugene eventually decided to realize his lifelong dream of coming to Israel. At age thirty-six, he was able to make *aliyah* through *The Fellowship*'s On Wings of Eagles program.

Moreover, Eugene was able to learn Hebrew in *Wings*-sponsored language classes—part of *The Fellowship*'s commitment to meeting immigrants' *klitah* (re-settlement) needs.

Eugene loves life in his new home and has high hopes for his future. In Russia, he was afraid to reveal his faith. But now, he holds his head high.

International Fellowship of Christians and Jews

BEING A PART OF HISTORY

John and Jennifer Rainney, Arizona

AN AMBITIOUS YOUNG man from Michigan, John Rainney set out early in life to make his own fun and fortune. He began by buying a franchise in the cleaning industry, after which he developed his own company that became quite successful. At the age of twenty-two, he was featured in a magazine as one of a handful of top young entrepreneurs in his city. He later partnered with a group of doctors and helped their restaurant venture succeed.

John eventually developed his gift of management into a niche in the food industry, and became a successful consultant—helping faltering businesses become profitable. "Although success is always sweet at first, it can turn sour," he shares. "I found myself working seven days a week, totally absorbed in the business. At one point I asked myself, 'Is this all there is to life?'"

That question lead to an epiphany for the driven young man. John decided to take a year off and travel. Jennifer, then his girlfriend, was at his side. He recalls, "It was a great time of reflection. We camped, hiked, meditated, and eventually came to the end of our road and resources in Arizona." When the money ran out, Jennifer went back to Michigan to find work in an area where she had friends and family. Though John had relatives in Arizona, he chose to live out of his car (albeit a nice one!) for several weeks until he was ready to dive back into the workforce. "My life to that point had been so shallow . . . so empty. I knew I needed God. I had gone to church in the past. I had always believed in God. I just took a long time sowing my wild oats."

In his early thirties, John began to seek God and to work in the trucking industry for well-known, national food distributors. He also recalls, "I was so in love with Jennifer, but I didn't think I was ready for marriage yet. Finally, she asked *me*!"

Today, the Rainneys have been married twelve years and are the owners of a successful trucking business that serves food distributors. John affirms, "Jennifer is just as responsible for our success as I am. We are equal partners." They are also partners in parenting two spectacular little girls, Rebecca and Meagan.

As God has blessed John and Jennifer personally and financially, they have nurtured a deep desire to bless the Jewish people. "I had worked with many Jews in our industry, and I loved them. They were typically people of great integrity and were very personable and likable," says John. "Rabbi Eckstein inspired us, and all that Jennifer and I do for the Jews, we do out of love. We have no interest whatsoever in recognition here on earth. Our reward is the joy we feel by giving out of love. Mother Theresa of Calcutta once said, 'Love in action produces good things.' We have found that to be so true."

"The time is short," says John emphatically. "What other people have been without a homeland for 2,000 years and then have been given it back—just as the scriptures predicted? What a joy to be a part of history through this ministry, to see God's chosen people gathered back into their rightful place!"

Sophie, Israel

Twenty-five years ago, Sophie and her family lived under anti-Semitic persecution in the Ukraine. She and her husband knew the only way to ensure their children's future was to move to Israel.

Sophie escaped to Israel with her boys, but her husband was forced to stay behind. Though she was heartbroken, she knew she had done the right thing for her children. She worked in a furniture store until age sixty-five when the store went bankrupt.

Sophie's sole source of income today is a small pension. Fortunately, she discovered *The Fellowship*'s *Chasdei Yosef* soup kitchen; otherwise, she might have had to live out her later years in poverty and isolation. "Thank God for all the people who make it possible," she says. "They are doing God's work. I am sure of this."

CALLED TO PRAY AND GIVE

Sandy Fox, Nebraska

SANDY FOX HAS lived most of her sixty years in Callaway, Nebraska, a town of only six hundred residents. She was raised on a farm nearby, where her family produced wheat and corn. As a child, she remembers the cows, sheep, and chickens that often ended up on the family dinner table! Cats and a dog were always a part of the landscape, too. Much to Sandy's childhood delight, her father's philosophy on cats and dogs was simple: "As long as they help keep the pest population down, they are welcome."

At the tender age of eighteen, Sandy married and started a family. In time, she had four children, and though the family moved a lot, they somehow kept coming back to Callaway. Ultimately, Sandy invested over twenty-five years in her profession as a nurse's aide. "It's one of the hardest jobs among those that are traditionally thought of as women's jobs," says the seasoned veteran. "I'm just now going into 'semi-retirement,' because I feel God is saying it's time, and I'm not as strong as I used to be!"

Sandy understands the important link between Christians and the Jewish people. At one point, God brought a Jewish friend into Sandy's life. Sandy recalls that this neighbor often invited her and her children over for Friday evening Shabbat. Later in life, Sandy attended a church that celebrated Jewish heritage and customs as they relate to Christianity—further deepening her connection to God and the Jewish people. "I believe our deepest calling from God is simply to pray God's blessing on the Jewish people and to be great friends to them," she says.

Then one day while watching *On Wings of Eagles* on television, Sandy sensed that God wanted her to pray about giving. It was a true dilemma, for her income was small, and she already was giving to several other ministries. Even so, she couldn't deny the tug on her heart, and she began to give.

As Sandy's connection to *The Fellowship* strengthened, her desire to give only grew stronger. Given her background in working with the elderly, Sandy was especially moved by the prospect of helping elderly Jews from Russia make safe passage to Israel. "It's so wonderful to be a part of helping them once they get there, too," she says with genuine joy.

Over time, Sandy was able to save some money and make a special, substantial gift. But she is praying that this is only the beginning. "I know this sounds crazy, but I have such boldness to ask God to enable me to give thousands, hundreds of thousands, or even millions one day to *The Fellowship*. It seems impossible, but with God, all things can become possible."

Marcos & Zola

In South America, the threat of physical harm due to anti-Semitism is never far away. Marcos and Zola, a brother and sister in Ecuador, feared for their safety and the future of Zola's two sons. So they decided to move to Israel, their biblical homeland.

Through a *Fellowship*-funded absorption center in the city of Be'er Sheva, Marcos and Zola found much-needed assistance and a place to live. The center serves over 3,000 new immigrants annually, helping them adjust to life in Israel.

Zola joyfully says, "My children now have a real future. Here many kind people are helping them—and they are *happy*! We are so grateful."

ow good and pleasant it is when brothers live together

in unity! . . . For there the LORD bestows his blessing, even

life forevermore.

PSALM 133:1, 5

wo are better than one, because they have a good return

for their work: If one falls down, his friend can help him up.

But pity the man who falls and has no one to help him up!

Though one may be overpowered, two can defend themselves.

A cord of three strands is not quickly broken.

ECCLESIASTES 4:9-10, 12

FULFILLING GOD'S PURPOSES

Varitema Tema Nasau, California

BORN IN THE beautiful Fiji Islands in the South Pacific, Varitema Tema Nasau was the second oldest of seven children and was raised by her Christian grandparents in a farming community. Gentle and laid back, she is one who laughs easily and has a tremendously tender heart toward people in need.

"I was so blessed growing up," relays Varitema, with genuine joy in her voice. "My grandparents grew peanuts, rice, yams, and other native vegetables, and the children got to help. I was kind of a tomboy, so it was wonderful for me." She laughs heartily and adds, "We even rode wild, native horses bareback to the market!"

As a young girl, Varitema recalls having a keen interest in world news. "I would sneak away with my grandfather's newspaper and read," she recalls. In those days, the radio was the young girl's "best friend." As she listened to it, she was especially dismayed by events taking place in Israel. "I remember crying, sobbing even, as I saw the Israeli soldiers trying to protect the small country. I knew from reading the Bible that the Jews were God's chosen people. It just broke my heart that they had such fierce enemies."

Native Fijians are largely Christian by faith, with many belonging to the Methodist denomination. Varitema believes that God had His hand on her even as a child so that she could be a part of fulfilling His purposes later in life.

While in high school, Varitema's God-given gift of compassion led her into mission work. She joined *Youth with a Mission* and served in Australia among the aborigines, and then came to the United States, landing in the San Francisco Bay Area. "I had an auntie who lived there," she says. "While I was there, I attended a church and took teens out to help street people—providing food, blankets in winter, and other necessities."

Now in her forties, Varitema has had a long career as a live-in caretaker. "God has blessed me so much," she says, her voice brimming with gratitude. "I remember receiving a mailing about *The Fellowship*. My heart went out to these people the moment I heard what they are going through. I prayed, 'God, please let me help!'" Holding back tears, she recalls the compassion she felt for the Jewish people: "I asked God . . . " She pauses momentarily and then regains her voice, "I asked Him, 'Let me get one Jew home every month from my paycheck!'"

A single woman with a willing heart and strong work ethic, Varitema has become an amazing giver from all that God has provided. She is more than delighted and "privileged" to help with any needs through *The Fellowship*. "I want to help in every way—whether it's in the soup kitchen or the bomb shelters, with children or the elderly," she says.

Varitema urges Christians everywhere to pray for the peace of Jerusalem. "God is so big. So *real*," she says with wonder. "We must never forget to pray for Israel. If we will pray, God will hear us and answer our prayers for our brothers and sisters there."

Victor, Ukraine

Victor, a ten-year-old boy, lived in Melitopol, Ukraine. His mother, Anna, did all she could to support her son, but her work kept her away from home. Victor often wandered the streets without supervision.

When pipes broke in their tiny apartment, Anna could not afford to have the water damage repaired. Their damp home, combined with malnutrition, made both mother and child ill.

One day, a coworker told Anna about the *Warm Home* for boys in the nearby city of Donetsk, funded by the *Fellowship's Isaiah 58* program. There, at-risk boys like Victor receive hot meals, good secondhand clothing, and a warm bed to sleep in.

The *Warm Home* is just what Victor needed—a stable environment, direct supervision from caring adults, and the good nutrition he needs to stay healthy.

International Fellowship of Christians and Jews

INSPIRING A LEGACY OF LOVE

David & Dianna Shipley, Tennessee

When Dianna Shipley was a young teenager, she spent summers washing dishes at the local country club. Adopted as an infant by "wonderful" parents, Dianna especially enjoyed her summer job because she was often able to see her father who was an avid golfer.

With both her parents being solid Christians, Dianna was introduced to a charismatic church when she was around thirteen years old. Her faith grew and "never wavered." Her love and respect for the scriptures helped her realize, even at a young age, that the Jews were God's chosen people.

One summer when Dianna was seventeen, she spotted a handsome "older man" (in his early twenties). He was helping park golf carts at the country club. Providentially, both young adults met at a mutual friend's home. "We hit if off right away!" Dianna reminisces, still almost giddy at the memory.

After high school, Dianna attended medical school while David worked for a bank. Once they were married, she invited David to church. "I knew I needed God," he recalls with reverence. "I went down to the altar and dedicated my heart to His service."

Soon, the couple was blessed to welcome their son, Jonathan, to their lives. About that same time, Dianna was about to begin her residency, and David's bank went through a management change that resulted in his being laid off.

"Here we had this amazing gift of our son," recalls David, "and yet I was unemployed and wondering what to do next." Dianna wisely suggested that they consider having David care for Jonathan during the hours when she would be in the residency program. "It turned out to be the best fit for everyone," says David with fatherly pride. "And it wasn't too long before we added our daughter, Emily, to our family."

David homeschools both children. "He has always been great with the kids," relates Dianna. "I remember seeing signs all over the house with words on them—like the word *sit*, taped to a chair. I was so proud of what David was doing for our family and grateful for his support of my career in medicine." After completing eleven years of medical school and residencies, Dianna became an oncologist.

It was David who first heard about *The Fellowship*, having seen *On Wings of Eagles* on television. "I have always been amazed at the transformation that took place in Israel. In a short time, this tiny country the size of New Jersey went from being a wasteland to flourishing with natural resources—the result of work done by some of the best scientists in the world," he says. He and Dianna have had the privilege of taking their children to special gatherings at the Israeli embassy for Christians who support Israel. The visits were an exhilarating experience for Jonathan and Emily, who are studying the nation's remarkable history.

The couple is eager to let the Jews in Israel know that Christians in America care deeply about them. "We are so honored and blessed to have even a small role in re-gathering God's people from different parts of the earth," says David. Dianna adds with conviction, "It's hard for Americans to understand that Jewish families live in constant threat of attack. We want them to know they are not alone."

Ziv, Israel

As a boy in Ethiopia, Ziv dreamed of coming to Israel. "I didn't know the names of cities in Ethiopia—but I knew the city of Jerusalem!" he laughs.

Years later, Ziv's dream became a reality when *On Wings of Eagles* helped him make *aliyah* with his family. But life wasn't easy at first. His parents couldn't find work, and after Ziv served in the Israeli military, he couldn't find work either.

But eventually all that changed. Through a *Fellowship*-funded program that equips young Ethiopian immigrants with computer skills, Ziv broke the cycle of poverty. Though his studies challenged him, Ziv graduated successfully, and now he'll be able to get a good job and support his aging mother and father.

ADOPTED INTO GOD'S FAMILY

Charlotte Karl, Alabama

CHARLOTTE "MAWMAW" KARL is the consummate southern grandmother—a true "lady," whose strength is tempered by love and whose determination is driven by conviction. Her captivating southern accent is so endearing that one immediately feels at home when talking with her.

Home is in fact where Charlotte shines best. The mother of three grown children, she has made it a life-priority to bond with her five grandchildren—one boy and four girls, ranging in age from three to fifteen. "It amazes me that the teenagers still want to come to my house and sleep over. I just love it!" laughs MawMaw. "The older ones actually bicker about who's going to come next. There's no higher compliment than that for *this* grandma!"

Charlotte is also a late-in-life newlywed who loves to steal away for a quiet dinner with her husband. "Years before we met, my husband and I had grieved the loss of our spouses the same year," she relays. "When we met, we became fast friends. We are so blessed to be sharing this stage in life together."

Love of family is ingrained in Charlotte and is no doubt part of the reason she has felt "called" to give to the Jewish people. "Christians have been adopted into God's family through the Jews," says Charlotte. With great enthusiasm, she then adds, "It is *wonderful* to be able to love them and be a part of God's plan for the nation of Israel."

Charlotte first learned of *The Fellowship* by seeing a presentation of *On Wings of Eagles*. "I was moved to tears," she remembers, "yet it was much more than just an emotional experience. I knew I had to *do* something. It was truly a call of God on my life."

Needing to sell her home after the death of her former husband, Charlotte promised a portion of the proceeds to God if He would help her sell the property quickly. "My money is God's money anyway," says Charlotte. "And would you believe it? I had an offer in two weeks!" God has blessed Charlotte on two other occasions with the sale of property. Each time, she could hardly wait to write checks to help more Jews in need. "The worst thing I can think of when faced with great needs that weigh on our hearts, is not having the ability to do something about it," conveys Charlotte with sincerity. "I am absolutely amazed that the Creator of the universe chooses to use people who are selfish by nature to alleviate the needs of others. I've experienced such joy in being able to be a small part of His plans that I am thrilled to give. This has been a calling for me. I am so excited to see biblical prophecy fulfilled."

Victoria, Israel

Victoria's parents often discussed making *aliyah* from their native Russia. As a teenager, she took a short trip to the Holy Land. Deeply moved, she resolved that someday she would live there. "There was something about Israel that made me feel like it was home," she says.

Years later, Victoria's dream of living in Israel was finally realized with the help of *The Fellowship*'s *On Wings of Eagles* program. Once there, Victoria went to a *Wings*-sponsored absorption center to receive job and language training.

She misses her parents, but is overjoyed to be in Israel—it has renewed her Jewish faith and given her the strength and courage to face her challenges. "My parents miss me too, but they know Israel is the future of the Jewish people," she says. "They hope one day to come and join me."

A FAMILY AFFAIR

Dana Kent & Scott Sears Family, Virginia

Dana Kent recently had to have her cat, Steven, put down after an almost twenty-year relationship. She's still healing emotionally, as are her family and two black Labradors who miss Stevie's comforting presence.

Although this event is not extraordinary to animal-loving families, it was a bit more difficult in this instance, because both Dana and her husband, Scott, are veterinarians. Scott had to administer the injection. "I just couldn't do it," recalls Dana. "It was really tough."

"Our accountant is Jewish and treats us like family," Dana explains. "He and his wife sent us a card that shared their tradition of planting something living in memory of someone lost. So it seemed fitting to them that one of God's creatures that had lived a full, long life should have a tree planted in Israel in the Children's Forest."

Dana has had a long-term love for Jews and Israel. "My grandmother, my mother, and I have always had a passion for prophecy and for the Jewish people," she says. "Scott and I especially enjoy listening to Christian teachers who are masterful at bringing out the Jewish point of view. This is so critical to understanding the richness of our own faith and even the scriptures themselves. Sadly, the Christian and Jewish connection is often overlooked by many churches."

Scott and Dana met in veterinary school. "I kept my maiden name because as long as I can remember, I wanted to be a vet, and I had a lifelong dream of becoming 'Dr. Kent.'"

Dana had another dream of one day hugging a lion. She thought she'd have to wait for heaven to see that one come to pass. But during an internship in college, a lion was brought in for treatment. "Of course we sedated him, but I have a picture hanging on my clinic wall of me with my arms around that lion's neck!"

Now married sixteen years, Scott and Dana have shared their support of the Jewish people with their children, Caleb, age twelve, and Katie, age nine. In fact, the children help out during the summer, for pay, at Dana's veterinary clinic. "One summer Caleb and Katie decided to save 10 percent, or 'God's money,' in a special charity box for Israeli orphans," recalls Dana. When they sent the donation at summer's end, the children were excited to include a picture of themselves holding the box.

For big-hearted dreamers like Dana and Scott, *The Fellowship* has provided a way to "give the Israeli people immediate relief and real hope for a bright future." Says Dana, "Not only can these people be removed from anti-Semitic countries, but also, through the programs of *The Fellowship*, they will have all they need to integrate into society when they reach their promised land."

Dana and Scott stand firm in their commitment to contribute toward such lasting change. It is little wonder that they are passing on their convictions to their children, helping them carry on the family legacy of love, respect, and faith in action.

Marko, Israel

When Marko was only seven, his mother died, and he was sent to live in an orphanage. Deep in grief, he became angry and defiant. He also suffered from an undiagnosed learning disability and did poorly in school.

Fortunately, the *Tuvia Community*, funded by *Guardians of Israel*, offers a loving environment where traumatized children can find healing.

Staff at the home treated Marko with compassion, patiently teaching him to act more responsibly. He soon enjoyed working on the orphanage farm, and developed a positive attitude. His learning disability was diagnosed and his schoolwork improved. Now eighteen, he will graduate from high school and go on to serve in the military. Marko is genuinely grateful, for he knows how close he came to life on the streets.

GIVING AND RECEIVING

Jay and Jo Anne Gould, West Virginia

A DYNAMIC COUPLE with big hearts, Jay and Jo Anne Gould were born and raised in the mountainous state of West Virginia. Having raised three children, they now revel in the joy their four grandchildren and one great-grandchild bring to their lives.

Jay is an electrical engineer who developed a niche in repairing machinery that is used in conjunction with the mining industry. Jo Anne helped Jay with the bookkeeping and administrative tasks of the business.

One day, while keeping up with office work, Jo Anne left the television on in the background. "All of a sudden, there was Rabbi Eckstein talking about *The Fellowship*," she says. "I have a real empathy for any people group facing discrimination. I really felt the world should be large enough for the Jewish people. They have suffered enough."

Jay and Jo Anne are wise stewards of their finances and like to make sure that organizations will use their money with true integrity. While researching this aspect of *The Fellowship* before making a donation, the Goulds received four checks—all from unexpected sources—in one day. The most amazing part of this event was that the amount was equal to the figure Jo Anne already had in mind to give to *The Fellowship*. She had set her heart on sending one Jew home per Gould family member. Jay affirms her enthusiasm when he says, "It became pretty clear to us that God wanted us to give to the Jewish people!"

This was just the beginning of the "bless fest" that God orchestrated between needy, hurting Jews and Jay and Jo Anne. The couple gave to all aspects of *The Fellowship*'s ministry—from food boxes, to orphanages, to bringing Jews back to Israel.

Relays Jay, "A floodgate of blessings opened for our family in a very short period of time. Our adult children received pay raises, our granddaughter who had severe food allergies was healed, and many other spiritual and emotional healings took place throughout our immediate and extended family."

An avid student of Judaica, Jay owns a Babylonian Talmud and an *Encyclopedia of Judaica*. "I have been amazed at recent discoveries of the 'lost tribes' of Israel. They validate scripture prophecies that are 2,700 years old!" he says. "It's beyond exciting to be a part of bringing them back to their homeland."

The Goulds have traveled extensively, most recently with *The Fellowship* on a trip to Israel. "Being in the Holy Land is a profound experience," says Jo Anne. "If Christians have the opportunity to someday pray at the Wailing Wall, with all my heart, I encourage them to do so."

Misha, Kiev

Nine-year-old Misha had been living in an orphanage in the Ukraine since his mother abandoned him at birth. Because of limited care, he eventually became sickly and required constant medical attention. Fortunately, his frail great-grandmother learned of the *Orach Chaim* children's home, funded by *The Fellowship*'s *Isaiah 58* program.

Misha entered the home, and the staff provided a balanced diet and made sure he attended school. A bright boy now in second grade, he has recovered his strength, does well in his studies, and participates in activities with the other children.

This little boy's future was bleak until he was "adopted" by caring *Isaiah 58* friends who help so many children with no one to look out for them.

If you spend yourselves in behalf of the hungry and satisfy the needs of the oppressed, then your light will rise in the darkness, and your night will become like the noonday.

The LORD will guide you always; he will satisfy your needs in a

sun-scorched land and will strengthen your frame. You will be

like a well-watered garden, like a spring whose waters never fail.

ISAIAH 58:10-11